And now to him who can keep you on your feet,
standing tall in his bright presence,
fresh and celebrating — to our one God,
our only Savior, through Jesus Christ, our Master,
be glory, majesty, strength, and rule before all time,
and now, and to the end of all time. Yes.

Jude 1:24–25 (MSG)

Scripture quotations marked CEV are taken from the Contemporary English Version. Copyright
© 1991, 1992, 1995 by The American Bible Society. Used by permission.

Scripture quotations marked NCV are taken from the New Century Version®. Copyright ©
2005 by Thomas Nelson, Inc. Used by permission. All rights reserved.

Scripture quotations marked MSG are taken from The Message: The Bible in Contemporary
Language. Copyright © by Eugene H. Peterson 1993, 1994, 1995, 1996, 2000, 2001, 2002.
Used by permission of NavPress Publishing Group.

Scripture quotations marked NIV are taken from the Holy Bible: New International Version
(North American Edition)®. Copyright © 1973, 1978, 1984 by International Bible Society.
Used by permission of Zondervan Publishing House. The "NIV" and "New International Version"
trademarks are registered in the United States Patent and Trademark Office by International
Bible Society.

Scriptures marked NLT are from the New Living Translation® of the Bible, copyright © 1996,
2004, 2007 by Tyndale House Publishers. Used by permission. All rights reserved. New Living
Translation® and its logo are registered trademarks of Tyndale House Publishers, Inc.

Editorial Director: Theresa Trinder
Art Director: Kevin Swanson
Designer: The DesignWorks Group
Back cover image: Steve Gardner, Pixelworks Studios, Inc.

ISBN: 978-1-59530-478-0
BOK3200

Printed and bound in China

promises and prayers

for your CONFIRMATION

Congratulations!

Congratulations, you've been confirmed! That means you've taken a very important step in your faith. It means you've decided to take everything you've been taught about God so far and make some pretty important decisions on your own. From now on, you and God will continue to build a relationship together as Father and child. Jesus will continue to show Himself as the truest friend you could ever hope to have. And you'll learn to hear and understand the Holy Spirit in your heart as you grow, make decisions, and deepen your faith.

Don't worry, though. You don't have to have all the answers now. Becoming who God created us to be takes a whole entire lifetime and then some. And knowing how bumpy the road can be sometimes, God gives us shock absorbers — encouragement through the words, music, and art of others who have experienced the things we're going through.

This book is full of the evidence of God's presence and love on this earth. The people who share themselves in these pages can relate to the joy, challenge, and excitement of seeking God. You can be sure you're not alone. Use this book as a reminder of that — and add your own thoughts in the margins, if you want. After all, you've been confirmed in your faith — God has big plans for you, and your road trip has already started!

Table of Contents

Blessings Are Everywhere

If you sometimes stop to notice the subtly beautiful things in life — like how good a compliment makes you feel, how awesome a blue sky polka-dotted with white clouds is, or that feeling in your stomach when you stand safely on the edge of a steep drop-off — then you know what blessings are. God fills the world with wonderful things for us. And the neat thing is, as soon as we recognize and appreciate one of them, it becomes a blessing for us. We don't have to wait for BIG things, like winning the lottery or being healed from sickness. If we're open to them, our hearts can be filled up every day with small reminders that God is with us and for us and full of love for us. Sometimes it's easy to forget how easy it is to be blessed by God!

*From the fullness of his grace
we have all received one blessing
after another.*

John 1:16 (NIV)

Not what we say about our blessings,
but how we use them, is the
true measure of our thanksgiving.

W.T. Purkiser

Prayers go up and blessings come down.

Yiddish proverb

However many blessings we expect from God,
His infinite liberality will always exceed all
our wishes and our thoughts.

John Calvin

Character Comes From Faith

Only God knows who He made each of us to be. Our quirks, our looks, our gifts and weaknesses are all important parts of our development into godly people. For that reason alone, comparing ourselves to others just doesn't make sense. The only comparison that really works is between ourselves and who God asks us to become. As we learn to focus less on what the world says is cool and more on God's word — when we start living by a different standard than most — we develop good character. Character is made up of big words like honesty, integrity, and courage. And since God made us to be full of character, we can be sure we have the ability in us to be all of those things and more!

The LORD does not look at the things man looks at. Man looks at the outward appearance but the LORD looks at the heart.

1 Sam. 16:7 (NIV)

I think people look more closely at our actions in the rough times, when the emotions are raw and our guard is down. That's when our true character shows and we find out if our faith is real. If I'm going to call myself a Christian, I have to honor Jesus in disappointments, too.

Tony Dungy, QUIET STRENGTH

Character is what you are in the dark.

D.L. Moody

Mom would always tell me, "Jackie, no matter what, always strive to be a good person." From her I learned that whatever you do is a test of character, a test of heart. Will you choose a godly path, or your own?

Jackie Joyner-Kersee, *TODAY'S CHRISTIAN WOMAN* INTERVIEW

Whatever you are, be a good one.

Abraham Lincoln

Charity Means Love

One definition of charity, according to the Random House Unabridged Dictionary, is "Christian love; agape." *Agape* (pronounced a-GA-pay) is one of three Greek translations for the word "love." *Agape* is an action. It means physically doing something to show love to another person. You don't have to *feel* kind toward someone in order to act. When we represent God by doing things that others might not be willing to do, we call attention to God's work in, and plan for, the world. It's this kind of action, often in places of obvious need, that makes other people sit up and notice. And the neat thing is, when we do something kind for someone else, for God's sake, He often thanks us by giving us those feelings of love and joy that we might not have started out with.

And if anyone gives even a cup of cold water
to one of these little ones because
he is my disciple,
I tell you the truth, he will certainly
not lose his reward.

Matt. 10:42 (NIV)

To ease another's heartache is to forget one's own.

Abraham Lincoln

When you carry out acts of kindness you get a wonderful feeling inside. It is as though something inside your body responds and says, yes, this is how I ought to feel.

Harold Kushner

Church, a.k.a. the Human Body

Imagine if you woke up one day to find that your right foot had gone completely numb. It would make it a little difficult to get around, wouldn't it? Now imagine each person in the world as a right foot. Or a hand, a hip, a shoulder, or even a heart or stomach. God builds His church like that, using people as vital organs and working parts. He gives us each a purpose — yes, each of us, including you and me — that will help His kingdom come on the earth. Knowing that each one of us is essential to God's plan makes us both dependent on others — because it means we weren't designed to do it all — and responsible for something important! As a part of the church body, we matter to God.

*God is building a home. He's using us all —
irrespective of how we got here — in what he is
building. He used the apostles and prophets
for the foundation. Now he's using you,
fitting you in brick by brick, stone by stone,
with Christ Jesus as the cornerstone that
holds all the parts together. We see it taking
shape day after day — a holy temple built
by God, all of us built into it, a temple
in which God is quite at home.*

Eph. 2:19-21 (MSG)

Church isn't where you meet. Church isn't a building.
Church is what you do. Church is who you are.
Church is the human outworking of the person of Jesus Christ.
Let's not go to Church, let's be the Church.

Bridget Willard

Never doubt that a small group of thoughtful,
committed citizens can change the world. Indeed,
it is the only thing that ever has.

Margaret Mead

Has it ever occurred to you that one hundred pianos all tuned
to the same fork are automatically tuned to each other? So one
hundred worshippers meeting together, each one looking away
to Christ, are in heart nearer to each other than they could
possibly be were they to become "unity" conscious and turn
their eyes away from God to strive for closer fellowship. The
body becomes stronger as its members become healthier. The
whole church of God gains when the members that compose it
begin to seek a better and a higher life.

A.W. Tozer

Commitment Makes a Comeback

Peter sure loved Jesus, and it showed by his commitment.
Like when he got out of the boat and walked on the water.
Not many of us would be brave enough to try that! Or when
he saw Jesus on the shore and jumped into the water to
swim there because the boat wouldn't sail fast enough.
Even on the night before Jesus' crucifixion, when Peter
denied knowing Christ three times, he immediately felt
horrible and cried out for forgiveness. Commitment to God
doesn't mean being perfect and obedient all the time.
It means coming back to Him over and over again, trusting
in His mercy and unconditional love.

The eyes of the Lord search the whole earth
in order to strengthen those
whose hearts are fully committed to him.

2 Chron. 16:9 (NLT)

An ounce of performance is worth
a pound of promises.

Mae West

If we're going to be Christians, if we're going to be who we say
we are—followers of Christ—we've got to really dig into the Word
and seek Him. The Lord has really taught me through the last
couple of years that you find out things from Him through
His Word, through His Spirit speaking to you and also through
the affirmations of brothers and sisters, people who have gone
before us who are stronger in their faith. [You] really need
to dig deep into what you believe and find out why you believe
that. Don't just do it because of tradition or because it's
what you've always been taught, but because you believe it
yourself and because you searched it and have
sought God's face on it.

Mac Powell

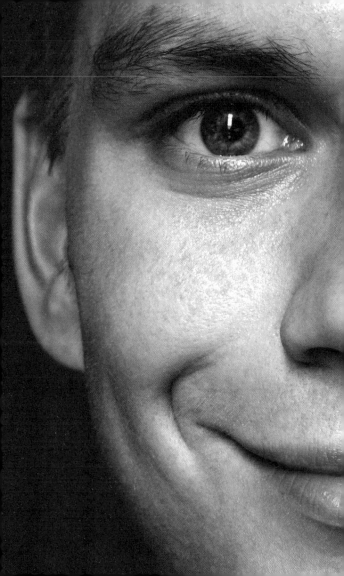

Communication Is More Than Words

Have you ever noticed how a smile is contagious? Try it sometime — smile at a complete stranger, and chances are they'll smile back without even thinking about it. We communicate with people all the time, through our facial expressions, body language, and words. How we interact with people sets the tone for our relationships with them — and tells people a lot about our attitude toward life. As children of God, we have the advantage of hope. And every day we can make the choice to demonstrate hope through a smile, a hug, or our willingness to listen to others. Communication is powerful!

May the words of my mouth
and the meditation of my heart
be pleasing in your sight,
O LORD, my Rock and my Redeemer.

Psalm 19:14 (NIV)

The most basic and powerful way to connect to another person is to listen. Just listen. Perhaps the most important thing we ever give each other is our attention . . . A loving silence often has far more power to heal and to connect than the most well-intentioned words.

Rachel Naomi Remen

Words which do not give the light of Christ increase the darkness.

Mother Teresa

Compassion Takes Action

Compassion means feeling pain in your heart that someone is suffering, and wanting to help them. It means putting yourself in their shoes and even being willing to walk *with* them for a while as you work together to solve a problem. Jesus did this when He gave up His personal time in order to preach to the thousands that had followed Him. The Good Samaritan went out of his way to pay for the treatment of a beat-up stranger. The rescue workers who helped at the World Trade Centers, and the countless people who helped rebuild New Orleans after Hurricane Katrina, have all showed deep compassion. If you ask God to open your eyes to it, there are chances to show compassion all over the place.

When he saw the crowds
he had compassion on them because
they were confused and helpless,
like sheep without a shepherd.

Matt. 9:36 (NLT)

If you can't feed a hundred people, then feed just one.

Mother Teresa

People need to see you're for real —
that you really care for them,
that you're even ready to put your life
on the edge for them.

Saul Cruz, LEADERSHIP MAGAZINE

Compassion [is] like seeing someone drowning in a river and
automatically you grab that person and save him. But as
you stand there, you see more and more people coming down
the river drowning and you just keep pulling them out.
Justice is when a person goes up the river to find the source of
the problem, to find out why these people are in the river in the
first place. They take what they see in front of them — people
drowning in the river — and their feet start moving. They
acquire knowledge in the process, and move from compassion
to justice. We need people downstream pulling people out,
[and] we need someone to get to the source of things.

David Crowder, CHRISTIANMUSICTODAY.COM INTERVIEW

Compassion will cure more sins
than condemnation.

Henry Ward Beecher

Contentment Takes Time to Learn

Happiness is momentary. It's a big feeling that doesn't last all that long, kind of like a burst of fireworks. Contentment doesn't feel as big, but it runs much deeper and lasts longer, like a burning candle. When you learn how to be content with what you have, contentment stays with you for a long, long time. It's not an easy thing to be satisfied with whatever you've been given — most adults struggle with it on a daily basis. And it doesn't mean you can't have goals and ambitions. It just means that you're grateful for God's blessings in your life and you recognize that you're going to be okay, no matter what. Contentment is lasting joy!

Serving God does make us very rich,
if we are satisfied with what we have.

1 Tim. 6:6 (NCV)

The secret of contentment is the realization
that life is a gift, not a right.

Author Unknown

True contentment is a real, even active, virtue —
not only affirmative but creative.
It is the power of getting out of any situation
all there is in it.

G.K. Chesterton

Being "contented" ought to mean in English what it does
in French, being pleased. Being content in an attic ought not to
mean being unable to move from it and resigned to living in it;
it ought to mean appreciating all there is in such a position.

G.K. Chesterton

Devotion to God

You yourself have shown devotion in more than one way. You're devoted to your family — loving them even when you're angry or upset and always coming back home at the end of the day. You've been devoted to schoolwork — maybe because you think you have to, but you still keep trying and have been for years. Devotion isn't about being perfect. It's about coming back, trying again; about loving, over and over again. It's about knowing where the lighthouse is and constantly aiming your strokes toward that light. It's about trusting that the man in the lighthouse will keep that light lit because he wants your journey to be safe. That's devotion — on your part and on God's.

Surrender your heart to God,
turn to him in prayer. . . .
Then you won't be ashamed;
you will be confident and fearless.
You will rest safe and secure,
filled with hope and emptied of worry.

Job 11:13, 15, 18 (CEV)

God always gives His best to those
who leave the choice with Him.

Jim Elliot

When a train goes through a tunnel and it gets dark,
you don't throw away the ticket and jump off.
You sit still and trust the engineer.

Corrie Ten Boom, *THE HIDING PLACE*

We are not built for ourselves, but for God.
Not for service for God, but for God.

Oswald Chambers

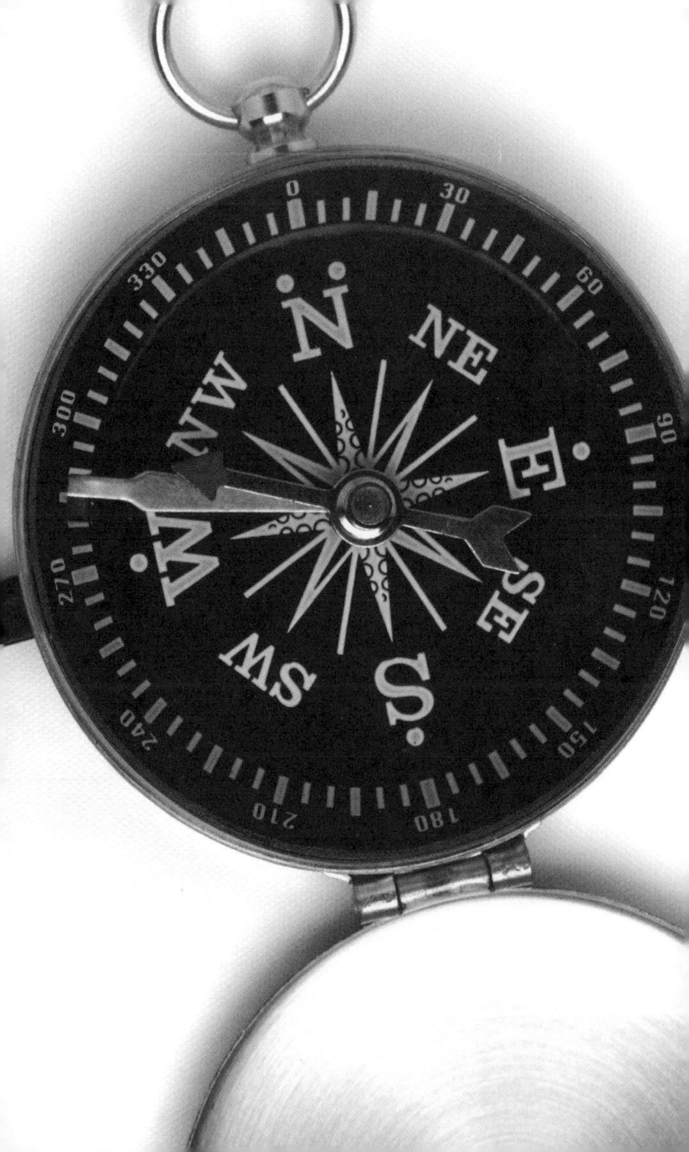

N
NE
E
SE
S
SW
W
NW
0
30
60
90
120
150
180
210
240
270
300
330

Discernment, or How to Read Your Compass

Navy ships use compasses to guide them. And when it's time to make sure the compass is set right, sailors take the ship to a quiet spot where they can drop anchor and really pay attention to what the compass is telling them. The compass inside us, which we call the Holy Spirit, also needs quiet space and time. The Holy Spirit whispers encouraging words to our hearts, helping us to make decisions. It's easy to miss His advice if we don't sit still and pay attention through prayer and listening. Learning to listen to the Holy Spirit takes patience, trying, and occasional mess-ups. But it's worth the work.

I pray that your love will keep on growing
and that you will fully know and understand
how to make the right choices. Then you will
still be pure and innocent when Christ returns.

Phil. 1:9-10 (CEV)

A good head and a good heart
are always a formidable combination.

Nelson Mandela

When one door closes, another opens;
but we often look so long and so regretfully upon the closed
door that we do not see the one which has opened for us.

Alexander Graham Bell

Evangelism 101

Do you have to stand on a street corner yelling to passersby, "Repent, for Jesus is near"? Absolutely not! Evangelism comes in all forms. It actually means to share the good news of Jesus Christ. And sharing can happen in lots of ways. If Jesus has given you an optimistic attitude, you can share encouragement with someone who's feeling low. If you get an allowance, you can buy a meal for a friend who forgot her lunch money. And if someone asks you what prompts you to be so kind, tell them you're just sharing what God gave you. That's evangelism — and it could literally change the life of someone you know.

*Always be prepared to give an answer
to everyone who asks you to give the reason
for the hope that you have.*

1 Pet. 3:15 (NIV)

*Evangelism is the spontaneous overflow of
a glad and free heart in Jesus Christ.*

Robert Munger

Any method of evangelism will work if God is in it.

Leonard Ravenhill

*Evangelism is not selling Jesus, but showing Jesus;
evangelism is not mere telling about Christ,
but about being Christ.*

Lee C. Camp, *MERE DISCIPLESHIP*

*Every life is a profession of faith, and exercises
an inevitable and silent propaganda.*

Henri Frédéric Amiel

Faith Is a Nightlight

You probably don't sleep with one now, but you may have when you were young. Nightlights aren't bright enough to keep you from sleeping. But if you happen to wake up when it's pitch black outside, when the whole house is silent and everyone else is in dreamland, that's when a nightlight seems like a little ray of hope. It's a promise that it won't be dark for very much longer — that the house still has electricity, and that if the bulb burns out, someone will change it. It's a reminder that someone cares a whole lot about you. That's what faith is. It's a promise that you can hold on to with all your might, that God loves you very, very much — and that you're never truly alone.

Faith is the confidence that what we hope for
will actually happen;
it gives us assurance about
things we cannot see.

Heb. 11:1 (NLT)

"I tell you the truth,
if you had faith even as small
as a mustard seed, you could say
to this mountain, 'Move from here to there,'
and it would move.
Nothing would be impossible."

Matt. 17:20 (NLT)

Doubts are actually a profound statement of faith because they're a person saying she won't let go of a good God in the face of the profound evil she's seeing.

Michael Card, *A SACRED SORROW*

A simple, childlike faith in a Divine Friend solves all the problems that come to us by land or sea.

Helen Keller

Every tomorrow has two handles. We can take hold of it with the handle of anxiety or the handle of faith.

Henry Ward Beecher

Faith sees the invisible, believes the unbelievable, and receives the impossible.

Corrie Ten Boom

Family Practice

In order to truly understand something, you've got to start from the beginning and learn. Family is kind of like that. From the minute we're born, we start learning what love is. God gives us parents, siblings, grandparents, and other family in order to help us understand how He Himself loves us. Of course, as we learn something new, we're not perfect at it. We mess up and make lots of mistakes. But that's okay! God knows we're sort of like rookies. We've got lots of potential, but we need time and a ton of practice. Loving our family — and seeing how they love us — is the best way to learn how much God loves us.

Think how much the Father loves us.
He loves us so much that he lets us be called
his children, as we truly are.

1 John 3:1 (CEV)

To us, family means putting your arms around each other and being there.

Barbara Bush

Acting is just a way of making a living, the family is life.

Denzel Washington

You don't choose your family.
They are God's gift to you, as you are to them.

Desmond Tutu

Family life is full of major and minor crises — the ups and downs of health, success and failure in career, marriage, and divorce — and all kinds of characters. It is tied to places and events and histories. With all of these felt details, life etches itself into memory and personality. It's difficult to imagine anything more nourishing to the soul.

Thomas Moore

Forgiveness – the Specialty of the House

It's hard to imagine this, but it's true: when we ask for forgiveness, no matter what we've done, God says yes! The even more amazing part is that once we've been forgiven, He never, ever holds it over our heads. He shows us by example what He wants us to do, for ourselves and for others. Forgiveness heals where revenge would make the pain worse. For us, sometimes it takes a really long time to *feel* love toward someone again once they've hurt us. But for God, it's instantaneous. After all, He's had a lot of practice. And if we ask Him for help, we'll learn to forgive, too.

I — yes, I alone —
will blot out your sins
for my own sake and will
never think of them again.

Isa. 43:25 (NLT)

Bear with each other and forgive whatever grievances you may have against one another. Forgive as the Lord forgave you.

Col. 3:13–14 (NIV)

God has a big eraser.

Billy Zeoli

To be a Christian means to forgive the inexcusable, because God has forgiven the inexcusable in you.

C.S. Lewis

To err is human; to forgive, divine.

Alexander Pope

God pardons like a mother, who kisses the offense into everlasting forgiveness.

George Herbert

Friends Are Little Jesus-Lessons

What would we do without them — the people in our lives who didn't come to us by blood, but by chance? Some friends come into our lives for a certain part of the trip. Others become lifelong loved ones we couldn't imagine ourselves without. Either way, friends help us to understand the type of love Jesus feels for us. As the best friend we could ever hope for, Jesus is perfect for confiding, sharing, and feeling connected. And our earthly friendships are made to help us understand what Jesus is all about. With that kind of sacred connection, isn't friendship neat?

Friends come and friends go, but a
true friend sticks by you like family.

Prov. 18:24 (MSG)

The only way to have a friend is to be one.

Ralph Waldo Emerson

Friendship is born at that moment when one person says to another: "What! You, too? I thought I was the only one."

C.S. Lewis

Love is the only force capable of transforming an enemy into friend.

Martin Luther King, Jr.

Friendship is precious, not only in the shade, but in the sunshine of life; and thanks to a benevolent arrangement of things, the greater part of life is sunshine.

Thomas Jefferson

Dolphins travel in groups called pods. These pods have always been a symbol for friendship to me because the dolphins really have fun with each other. But when one of them is injured or disoriented, two other dolphins immediately put their fins under the dolphin and bring it up to the surface so it can breathe. It's important to travel with friends who support and encourage each other in good and bad times.

Christina DiMari
TODAY'S CHRISTIAN WOMAN

Giving Freely Gives Freedom

Have you ever made juice, either from a can or from the fruit? Either way, the steps involve getting the juice from the source and pouring it into a glass. Once you have the juice, you drink it, taking in all the nutrients and vitamins that the fruit has to offer. Now what if the glass got greedy and didn't want to share its juice with you? God calls us to be vessels, like glasses of good things. He fills us up with so many blessings — ability, money, love, time, wisdom — with the intention of helping us to pour ourselves out to others, so that they can be nourished by God's love *through* us. When we help others, we improve the life of the one we help and we benefit from it ourselves. The more we give others, the more He gives us. When we are generous, we never have to worry about being empty of God's good blessings.

If you give to others,
you will be given a full amount
in return. It will be packed down,
shaken together, and spilling over
into your lap. The way you treat others is
the way you will be treated.

Luke 6:38 (CEV)

God has given us two hands —
one to receive with, and the other to give with.

Billy Graham

One verse in every six in the first three Gospels relates
either directly or indirectly to money. Sixteen of our Lord's
forty-four parables deal with the use or misuse of money.
A loving, joyful, liberal giving to the Lord's work is an
acid test of a spiritual heart, pleasing to God.

William Allen

You can give without loving,
but you cannot love without giving.

Amy Carmichael

The only things we can keep are the things
we freely give to God.

C. S. Lewis

God's Love Sticks Like Glue

Laminin is a glycoprotein found in the cells of every living thing. Basically, it's the glue that keeps us from falling apart. God's love is just like that. Once we accept Him, we can never, ever lose Him. His love seeps into every cell of us, wraps us up in it, and sticks to us like glue. Even when we're hurting or when someone tries to convince us that we're not lovable, we can know that is not true. Hear this: NO CHILD OF GOD IS UNLOVABLE. It's that simple. God loves us to pieces — pieces that are glued together by His very own hands.

And I am convinced that nothing can ever separate us from God's love. Neither death nor life, neither angels nor demons, neither our fears for today nor our worries about tomorrow — not even the powers of hell can separate us from God's love. No power in the sky above or in the earth below — indeed, nothing in all creation will ever be able to separate us from the love of God that is revealed in Christ Jesus our Lord.

Rom. 8:38-39 (NLT)

*I am not a theologian or a scholar, but I am very aware of
the fact that pain is necessary to all of us. In my own life,
I think I can honestly say that out of the deepest pain
has come the strongest conviction of the presence of God
and the love of God.*

Elisabeth Elliot, *GATEWAY TO JOY*

*The Christian does not think God will love us because
we are good, but that God will make us good
because He loves us; just as the roof of a sunhouse
does not attract the sun because it is bright,
but becomes bright because the sun shines on it.*

C.S. Lewis

God's Word: Show-and-Tell

"In the beginning was the Word," says the apostle John. "The Word was flesh, and it lived among us." But what does that mean? Imagine this: God loves us so much that He looks for ways to communicate with us, to help us understand His love for us. So He writes a whole big book to *explain* who He is. And He sends his very own son to the earth, to *show* who He is. The Bible and Jesus are God's own version of show-and-tell.

Your word is a lamp to my feet
and a light for my path.

Psalm 119:105 (NIV)

We must quit bending the Word to suit our situation.
It is we who must bend to that Word,
our necks that must bow under the yoke.

Elisabeth Elliot, *GATEWAY TO JOY*

Grace Is Full of Surprises

Grace is what happens when you're surprised with a gift you're not expecting. Like, what if your allowance were doubled one day, for no reason? What if you ordered a single scoop of chocolate on a cone and they gave you a triple scoop with sprinkles at no extra charge? Grace is God being generous with us just because He can — just because He wants to! He gives us more than we can give ourselves, because His power is limitless. God loves to give great surprises!

My grace is sufficient for you,
for my power is made perfect in weakness.

2 Cor. 12:9 (NIV)

*Grace is the love that takes us by surprise. It's the help
we hadn't counted on, the kindness we didn't think we deserved.
And maybe we don't, but it's there anyway.*

Lawrence Wood
ONE HUNDRED TONS OF ICE AND OTHER GOSPEL STORIES

*When we don't get what we deserve it's a real good thing—MERCY.
When we get what we don't deserve it's a real good thing—GRACE.
The consequences of God's grace are that we are forgiven,
restored, reconciled with God, given new life.*

Nigel James

*Grace means the free, unmerited, unexpected love of God,
and all the benefits, delights, and comforts which flow from it.
It means that while we were sinners and enemies
we have been treated as sons and heirs.*

R.P.C. Hanson

Thank you!

Gratitude Is a Cornerstone of America

Gratitude is such an important thing that there's a whole day dedicated to it! George Washington first suggested the idea of a national holiday of thanks. In 1863, in the midst of the Civil War, Abraham Lincoln suggested that a day of thanks be celebrated on the last Thursday of November. In 1941 Congress decided that the fourth Thursday of November be declared Thanksgiving Day, and it has been that way ever since. Every year the President of the United States makes a proclamation declaring the day.

It seems that gratitude is recognized as a very important thing. What are *you* grateful for?

Sing praises over everything,
any excuse for a song to God the Father in the
name of our Master, Jesus Christ.

Eph. 5:20 (MSG)

Always look at what you have left.
Never look at what you have lost.

Robert Schuller

Oh Lord, that lends me life,
lend me a heart replete with thankfulness.

William Shakespeare

Heaven — Like Earth, Only Way Better

Nobody has a clue what heaven will look like. Even if you were to picture your very, very best day on earth, with all of your dreams come true surrounding you, it would be like dust in the shadow of the beauty of heaven. All we know of heaven is that God has promised us a place there. Imagine that. What if He's there right now, vacuuming your carpet, putting your favorite candy in a jar on the dresser, buffing the chrome on your motorcycle. . . . Whatever your fantasies are, multiply them by a gazillion. Then know that in heaven, our earthly bodies will be gone and we will be the glorious, beautiful spiritual beings He has created us to be. What a thought. What a thing to look forward to!

*Even the world's best offer isn't worth nearly as much
as getting into heaven and hearing God say,
"Come into my kingdom, my good and faithful servant."
Hearing God say that is more
priceless than anything the world would have to offer.*

Leeland Mooring

CHRISTIANMUSICTODAY.COM INTERVIEW

Children are the hands by which we take hold of heaven.

Henry Ward Beecher

*What is heaven going to be like? Just as there is a mystery to
hell, so there is a mystery to heaven. Yet I believe the Bible
teaches that heaven is a literal place. Is it one of the stars?
I don't know. I can't even speculate. The Bible doesn't inform
us. I believe that out there in space where there are one
thousand million galaxies, each a hundred thousand light
years or more in diameter, God can find some place to put us
in heaven. I'm not worried about where it is. I know it is going
to be where Jesus is. Christians don't have to go around
discouraged and dependent with their shoulders bent.
Think of it — the joy, the peace, the sense of
forgiveness that He gives you, and then heaven too.*

Billy Graham

Holiness Trumps Perfection

A diamond is a diamond whether it's fresh from the mine, all cloudy and rough, or freshly set in a ring, all sparkling and clear. The difference is the process by which it is made into something beautiful. Either way, its worth is the same. Either way, the diamond expert sees it for what it is. It's much like that with us. We are beautiful creations, and God loves us, no matter what form we come to Him in, rough or smooth. The very act of coming to Him makes us holy — not perfect by our own count, but made perfect by His forgiveness and mercy. Trying to be perfect at anything is a waste of time, because we could never do that. But making holiness a goal, or letting God make us flawless, is a wonderful way to live.

At one time you were separated from God.
You were his enemies in your minds, and the
evil things you did were against God. But now
God has made you his friends again. He did this
through Christ's death in the body so that he
might bring you into God's presence as people
who are holy, with no wrong, and with nothing
of which God can judge you guilty. This will
happen if you continue strong and sure
in your faith. You must not be moved away
from the hope brought to you by the Good News
that you heard.

Col. 1:21-23 (NCV)

*Holiness has never been the driving force
of the majority. It is, however, mandatory for anyone
who wants to enter the kingdom.*

Elisabeth Elliot, *GATEWAY TO JOY*

*A holy life will make the deepest impression.
Lighthouses blow no horns, they just shine.*

Dwight L. Moody

*True holiness consists in
doing God's will with a smile.*

Mother Teresa

Integrity Is Total Trustworthiness

The word "integrity" comes from the same word that brings us "integer" — which, in math, means *whole*, like a whole number. So integrity means to be whole, complete, or sound. It means to know what your values are and to stick to them. Anytime you compromise your values, your integrity takes a hit. It's the "just this once" problem — like being offered a cigarette, and saying to yourself, "Just this once won't hurt." Or covering for a friend in a little white lie "just this once." When people start wondering if they can trust you, your integrity is in question. On the other hand, if you build a reputation of being totally trustworthy, that's one of the most valuable characteristics a person can have.

Someone will say, "You have faith; I have deeds." Show me your faith without deeds, and I will show you my faith by what I do.

James 2:18 (NIV)

Have the courage to say no. Have the courage to face the truth.
Do the right thing because it is right.
These are the magic keys to living your life with integrity.

W. Clement Stone

Your life may be the only Bible some people read.

Anonymous

Live in such a way that you would not be
ashamed to sell your parrot to the town gossip.

Will Rogers

Never give in! Never give in! Never, never, never, never—
in nothing great or small, large or petty. Never give in,
except to convictions of honor and good sense.

Winston Churchill

Jesus Is a Great Best Friend

Have you ever heard that old hymn "What a Friend We Have in Jesus"? The tune and language might be a little outdated, but the message is still true. While He was on earth, Jesus showed us the importance of being patient and a good listener and having trusted friends around us. He healed the sick, gave hope to the hopeless, stuck up for God's ways instead of empty rituals, and when it came down to Him or us . . . He died a horrible death so that we could live forever. And even though He isn't with us in human form anymore, His character hasn't changed a bit. Jesus is still all the things that make a wonderful friend. He's the best confidant. He's got a great sense of humor. And very best of all, following Him leads us straight into God's arms.

I am the light of the world.
Whoever follows me will never walk in
darkness, but will have the light of life.

John 8:12 (NIV)

I never really thought of the fact that Jesus calls "us" the light of the world. He is the ultimate light, but as we are here on this earth we are the representation of Christ. The Image of Him.

Jeremy Camp

The dearest friend on earth is a mere shadow compared to Jesus Christ.

Oswald Chambers

At the center of the Christian church for thousands of years has been this risen Christ who invites people to trust Him; trust him with life, trust Him with death, trust Him with sin, trust Him with future, trust Him with hope, trust Him with every day.

Rob Bell, BELIEFNET.COM INTERVIEW

You're born. You suffer. You die. Fortunately, there's a loophole.

Billy Graham

I saw the glory of God . . . saw it! And let me tell you that Jesus is alive . . . there's a living God, and I didn't even know it. I was wondering about it before, but now I'm not wondering. I know! And I thank God because there's a lot of people who think for sure . . . and some think maybe, or maybe not. But I know. God . . . I don't know . . . for some reason touched me, an old sinner.

George Foreman

Jesus: He'll Be Back

Jesus' time on earth was miraculous, to be sure. And before He left, He promised He'd be back to get us. Someday, when we're least expecting it, Jesus will return with fanfare. Satan's little stint on earth will be over. God will say to him, *all right, playtime's over. You're done torturing my children*. And we don't know what it will look like, but at that moment, Jesus will reclaim this earth and all of His brothers and sisters. From that moment on, all the pain and trouble we've had to learn to deal with will just disappear and we'll live in the kingdom of God as holy, happy, healthy spiritual people. Cool, huh? We have a lot to look forward to!

Yes, I'm on my way! I'll be there soon!
I'm bringing my payroll with me.
I'll pay all people in full for their life's work.

Rev. 22:12 (MSG)

Peter says in Acts, "He will return to restore everything." It is a giant thing that God is doing here. It is the reconciliation of all things. It is the putting back together of the whole universe how God originally intended it to be. One way to look at it is that the message is an invitation into God's giant, global, universal purposes that I actually get to be a part of. It is easy for it to become a very selfish thing—"look what I've got"— as opposed to "by the grace of God look at this amazing thing that He's been inviting people into for thousands of years." And that is quite an awe-inspiring, amazing thing.

Rob Bell, BELIEFNET.COM INTERVIEW

I'm living in the days ahead
I'm already dancing on the streets of gold
and I can't stop celebrating in my soul . . .
I'm living in the days ahead
Nothing on earth could ever compare
Can't wait 'til the day that I get there
When I see Jesus face to face . . .
What could be better?

33 Miles, *WHAT COULD BE BETTER (THE DAYS AHEAD)*

The Journey Is Worth It

As you get older, you start to realize that everything balances out. The good times are really good, and the rough times can be really rough. But when you put it all together, life is rich and wonderful. The awesome thing is that we have the best travel partner of all on the road of life. When we let God do the driving, we can trust that He won't steer us wrong.

Always let him lead you,
and he will clear the road for you to follow.

Prov. 3:6 (CEV)

Do not go where the path may lead;
go instead where there is no path and leave a trail.

Ralph Waldo Emerson

The secret of my success? It is simple. It is found in the Bible,
"In all thy ways acknowledge Him and He shall direct thy paths."

George Washington Carver

It's not the going out of port, but the coming in,
that determines the success of a voyage.

Henry Ward Beecher

The Master of Life's been good to me. He has given me strength
to face past illnesses, and victory in the face of defeat.
He has given me life and joy where others saw oblivion.
He has given new purpose to live for, new services to render and
old wounds to heal. Life and love go on, let the music play.

Johnny Cash

I'm thankful for what I've been through, because Romans 5:3–5
says "suffering produces perseverance; perseverance, character;
and character, hope." It's created such an intense hunger for the
Lord in me. And if I have to go through more to see Christ
continue to work in and through my life, I'm willing.

Shannon Ethridge
TODAY'S CHRISTIAN WOMAN

Kindness Is a Holy Banana

Kindness sounds easy, but it sure can be a chore. What about that kid in class who always picks on others or the girl who gossips about you or even a family member who's just getting on your nerves today? Not so easy to be kind then, is it? But here's the neat thing! The Bible actually says that kindness is one of the fruits of the spirit. In other words, the more you grow with God, the more fruit, or evidence of growth, others will see in you. That includes love, joy, peace, patience, kindness, gentleness, faithfulness, and self-control (Gal. 5:22–23 NIV). You don't have to be kind all of the time. But as you get to know Him, God will help you grow in kindness.

*Always try to be kind to each other
and to everyone else.*

1 Thess. 5:15 (NIV)

Let there be kindness in your face, in your eyes,
in your smile, in the warmth of your greeting. . . .
Don't only give your care, but give your heart as well.

Mother Teresa

Constant kindness can accomplish much.
As the sun makes ice melt, kindness causes misunderstanding,
mistrust, and hostility to evaporate.

Albert Schweitzer

Love and kindness are never wasted.
They always make a difference.
They bless the one who receives them,
and they bless you, the giver.

Barbara De Angelis

Laugh All You Want

God has given us a wonderful way to help heal ourselves physically, emotionally, and spiritually — it's called laughter. Laughing actually reduces the level of stress-producing hormones in your body. It also increases production of antibodies — those cells in you that fight off illness. Laughing is a healthy way to release emotions that would otherwise build up inside. And laughter is contagious. It's a great way to connect with others and lift their moods, too. Did you know you had such a powerful tool inside of you? Go ahead — laugh!

God has brought me laughter.

Gen. 21:6 (NIV)

A person without a sense of humor
is like a wagon without springs.
It's jolted by every pebble on the road.

Henry Ward Beecher

I am thankful for laughter,
except when milk comes out of my nose.

Woody Allen

Laughter is an instant vacation.

Milton Berle

Mirth is God's medicine. Everybody ought to bathe in it.

Henry Ward Beecher

Love in Action

The heart of God's plan for us is love. He loved us so much that He let His son *die* for us, because without that, we ourselves would have died. This is a huge concept that can be really hard to grasp. But to help us get it, God has given us the ability to love others and to be loved. People often assume love is a feeling. But if you read 1 Corinthians 13, count up the *action* words of love. Regardless of how someone feels, love can happen. Take a look at those around you—your friends, your family, and strangers— and see if you can see love in action.

Love is patient, love is kind. It does not envy, it does not boast, it is not proud. It is not rude, it is not self-seeking, it is not easily angered, it keeps no record of wrongs. Love does not delight in evil but rejoices with the truth. It always protects, always trusts, always hopes, always perseveres. Love never fails.

1 Cor. 13:4-8 (NIV)

And may you have the power to understand,
as all God's people should, how wide, how long, how high,
and how deep his love is.

Eph. 3:18 (NLT)

Love is a fruit in season at all times,
and within the reach of every hand.

Mother Teresa

In the absence of love,
there is nothing worth fighting for.

Elijah Wood

God proved His love on the cross.
When Christ hung, and bled, and died,
it was God saying to the world,
"I love you."

Billy Graham

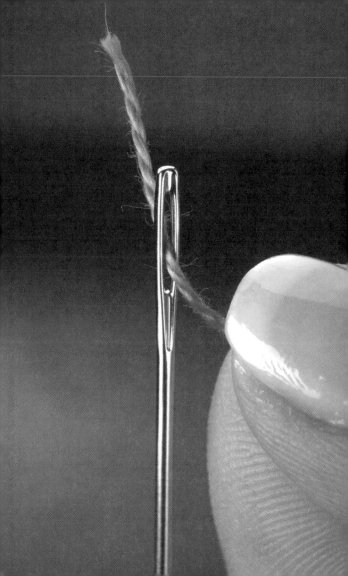

Maturity Happens One Thread at a Time

Chances are, your parents have commented at various times in your life on how grown-up you're getting. In fact, just completing confirmation is a big step toward maturity. And that's what it is—one step toward becoming who God made you to be. Life is all about *becoming*. You don't change who you are, like an aging chameleon —instead, each thread of your life is added to the tapestry that God is weaving for you. As you get older and more mature, the tapestry becomes more colorful and complete. And when it's time for you to go to heaven, however old you are, you'll be His special masterpiece.

He who began a good work in you
will carry it on to completion
until the day of Christ Jesus.

Phil. 1:6 (NIV)

Being a Christian is more than just an instantaneous conversion—it is
a daily process whereby you grow
to be more and more like Christ.

Billy Graham

A mature person is one who does not think only in absolutes,
who is able to be objective even when deeply stirred emotionally,
who has learned that there is both good and bad
in all people and all things,
and who walks humbly and deals charitably.

Eleanor Roosevelt

Maturity begins to grow when you can sense your
concern for others outweighing concern for yourself.

John MacNaughton

To make mistakes is human; to stumble is commonplace;
to be able to laugh at yourself is maturity.

William Arthur Ward

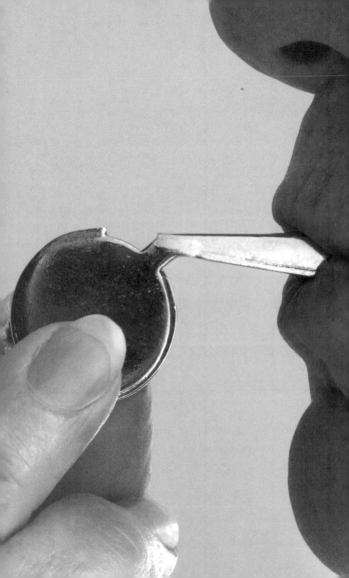

Obedience Takes Maturity

Now that doesn't sound like any fun, does it? Obedience is a hard thing to do all of the time. God gives us lots of places to practice, like with our parents, teachers, coaches, and pastors. A lot of the time obeying seems like the uncool thing. But really, obedience takes a lot of discipline and sometimes the ability to put what you know is the right thing ahead of your own feelings. And Jesus tells us that obeying our leaders is right, unless obeying would mean going against God. God wants us to know what it's like to live in freedom and joy. Obedience is a tool He's given us to learn how to do that — so a little pain now just might mean a whole lot of gain in the long run.

Serve only the Lord your God.
Respect him, keep his commands, and obey
him. Serve him and be loyal to him.

Deut. 13:4 (NCV)

*Anyone who hears and obeys these teachings of mine is like
a wise person who built a house on solid rock.
Rain poured down, rivers flooded, and winds beat against that
house. But it did not fall, because it was built on solid rock.*

Matt. 7:24–25 (CEV)

*What does it profit you to give God one thing
if He asks of you another? Consider what it is God wants,
and then do it. You will as a result better satisfy your heart
than with that toward which you yourself are inclined.*

St. John of the Cross

Perseverance Takes Practice

Have you practiced hard at a sport and won that big game? Have you studied for a really hard test and done well? Or have you sat there and eaten every last vegetable on your plate so you could have dessert? That's perseverance! It means not giving up, because you know the rewards will be great. Sports, school, family trials, and even vegetables can be ways He shows us how to get through things that are hard. The little difficulties can prepare us for bigger, tougher things, where the rewards are even greater. And ultimately, when we've lived our whole lives, we get the best reward of all — because God is at the finish line, waiting to hand us the grand prize.

In his kindness God called you to share
in his eternal glory by means of Christ Jesus.
So after you have suffered a little while,
he will restore, support, and strengthen you,
and he will place you on a firm foundation.

1 Pet. 5:10 (NLT)

So let's not allow ourselves to get fatigued doing good.
At the right time we will harvest a good crop if we
don't give up, or quit.

Gal. 6:9 (MSG)

God is with us. God is for us.
He won't ever abandon us.

Tony Dungy, QUIET STRENGTH

Here is the test to find whether
your mission on earth is finished:
if you're alive, it isn't.

Richard Bach

One cold February day, a snail started climbing an apple tree.
As he inched slowly upward, a worm stuck its head
from a crevice in the bark to offer some advice: "You're wasting
your energy. There isn't a single apple up there."
The snail kept up his slow climb.
"There will be when I get there," he said.

Anonymous

Prayer — Yes, He Can Hear You Now

Long before texting was invented . . . long before cell phones, regular phones, or even the Pony Express . . . people were using the most advanced form of communication that will ever be in existence. It's a direct, always-on, always-in-service-area line to God. Prayer isn't something that needs to happen at certain times or places. It's a way to stay connected to God all the time, no matter what you're doing. Can you imagine having instant access to your wisest mentor, your most caring nurturer, and your very best friend all at once? You've got it! Just hit speed dial to God.

I tell you, whatever you ask for in prayer,
believe that you have received it,
and it will be yours.

Mark 11:24 (NIV)

Never stop praying.

1 Thess. 5:17 (NLT)

Some people think God does not like to be troubled
with our constant coming and asking.
The way to trouble God is not to come at all.

D.L. Moody

When life knocks you to your knees, and it will, why, get up!
If it knocks you to your knees again, as it will, well,
isn't that the best position from which to pray?

Ethel Barrymore

Prayer is first of all listening to God. It's openness.
God is always speaking; He's always doing something.
Prayer is to enter into that activity.

Henri Nouwen

There are many things that are essential to arriving
at true peace of mind, and one of the most important is faith,
which cannot be acquired without prayer.

John Wooden

To be a Christian without prayer is no more possible
than to be alive without breathing.

Martin Luther King, Jr.

Priorities Are Everyday Choices

The fact that you're reading this book right now shows you've put getting closer to God ahead of any other thing you could be doing. You make similar choices all day, every day, whether you realize it or not. Even things that seem out of your control, like going to your least favorite class or doing some chore your parents have asked you to do, are actually totally up to you. If you do those things, you've chosen to put your education, your desire not to be punished, or obedience to your parents ahead of your other options. Every step you make shows God where your heart is.

He who pursues righteousness
and love finds life, prosperity and honor.

Prov. 21:21 (NIV)

I believe in person to person.
Every person is Christ for me,
and since there is only one Jesus,
that person is the one person in
the world at that moment.

Mother Teresa

God comes first. Paradise is not cheap.

Hakeem Olajuwon

Redemption Has Big Payoffs

One definition of the word *redemption*, according to the Random House Dictionary, is to repurchase, or to pay off. People basically go out and sell themselves for things they think will fill them up and make them happy. Looking anywhere but to God for joy just brings more emptiness. But we just keep trying. Fortunately, we have another option. When we see that going down the wrong path is actually more painful than we thought, we can ask God for help. And even though we've sold ourselves — our purity, our innocence, our childlike faith — through redemption, God buys us back. He pays off our spiritual debts and lets us start clean with Him. No grudges, no unforgiveness. Just a happy, loving God willing to give us second chances.

*You answered my prayer and came
when I was in need. You told me, "Don't worry!"
You rescued me and saved my life.*

Lam. 3:56-58 (CEV)

The law of my God is perfect. It condemns but forgives.
It restores — more than abundantly — what it takes away.

Jim Elliot

Just as a wounded starfish can mend
if thrown back into the ocean,
I learned my broken heart could mend
if I immersed myself in God.

Christina DiMari
TODAY'S CHRISTIAN WOMAN

We are God's very own, being redeemed by Him.
Every Christian therefore should wear a sign in his heart,
"Not for sale!"

Anonymous

To deliver us from evil is not merely to take us out of hell,
it is to take us into heaven.

P.T. Forsyth, **THE WORK OF CHRIST**

Relationship with God

It's hard to fathom that the Creator of the universe wants to have a relationship with us. How can He have the time, energy, interest, and patience to want to get to know each and every one of us personally — and let each of us get to know Him? Mind-boggling, isn't it? But the whole reason He made us was to show us love. And He gives us a whole lifetime to learn what that means. We don't have to have all the answers, because He already does. He just asks us to trust Him like we do our other loved ones.

Come near to God and
he will come near to you.

James 4:8 (NIV)

When you're in the presence of God,
I don't care who you are,
that's where everyone feels home.
That's how it was meant to be.

Leeland Mooring
CHRISTIANMUSICTODAY.COM INTERVIEW

The best of it is, God is with us.

John Wesley

God does not have to come and tell me what I must do for Him,
He brings me into a relationship with Himself where I hear His call
and understand what He wants me to do, and I do it out of
sheer love to Him. . . . When people say they have had a call
to foreign service or to any particular sphere of work, they
mean that their relationship to God has enabled them
to realize what they can do for God.

Oswald Chambers

Have you ever looked up in the nighttime sky and
wondered if God thinks about you? He knows you.
He hasn't forgotten you. He wants you to know him, too.

Christina DiMari
TODAY'S CHRISTIAN WOMAN

Responsibility Is in Your Hands

A mom had three sons who each had his own room. She asked them to keep their rooms clean for a whole month. The first son cleaned up once a week, ignoring a few Legos under the bed or a dirty sock in the corner. The second son took a few minutes each day to put things where they belonged. The third son waited until the day before the month was over and then shoved everything he owned into the closet. When the mom saw how her sons had cleaned, she took all the toys of the third son and gave them to the second son. "When you do so little with what I've given you, you'll get little back from me," she said. "But when you take care of what you have, you'll get more than you bargained for." How do you treat the things and responsibilities you've been given? What you do with God's gifts to you will affect how He'll bless you in the future. It's totally up to you.

The one who plants and the one who waters work together with the same purpose. And both will be rewarded for their own hard work.

1 Cor. 3:8 (NLT)

Be good, keep your feet dry, your eyes open,
your heart at peace and your soul in the joy of Christ.

Thomas Merton

Let everyone sweep in front of his own door,
and the whole world will be clean.

Johann Wolfgang von Goethe

Be the change you want to see in the world.

Mahatma Gandhi

You are not only responsible for what you say,
but also for what you do not say.

Martin Luther King, Jr.

Ask not what your country can do for you;
ask what you can do for your country.

John F. Kennedy

Salvation Comes From God

There is nothing you can do to make God love you less than He does. *Nothing*. Absolutely nothing will make God love you less than He loves you. And you know what? There's nothing you can do to make Him love you more, either. The simple beauty of being a believer in Christ is that when you ask for it, you're forgiven. You're saved. You can't do good deeds just to get on His good side, because you already *are* on His good side. And He already loves you more than you can possibly, humanly understand. Salvation comes from God alone — not from pleasing other people, not from doing good things, not from being a good student or sibling or daughter or son or person. When you follow Jesus, you're saved from any reason for embarrassment, shame, or remorse.

Everyone who believes in him
receives forgiveness of sins in his name.

Acts 10:43 (NIV)

*I'm fallen, human, needy, depraved, whatever you want
to call it. . . . But praise the Most High, that SO isn't the
end of the story! . . .
HIS strength be proved in my weakness.
HIS salvation seen within a messed up person.
HIS Spirit at work within an otherwise hopeless creature . . .
and inspiring a love for Jesus that overshadows everything else
and points undoubtedly to Another Place.*

Bethany Dillon

*It is the rightful heritage of every believer,
even the newest in the family of faith, to be absolutely certain
that eternal life is his present possession.*

Larry McGuill

Self-Image = God-Image

This is absolutely true: You are beautiful. You might not believe it, but you are. Sometimes it's hard for us to understand that concept — that each one of us is totally beautiful — because we see inside ourselves to the ugly things we think, feel, and do. But those things don't make us ugly. They make us completely normal human beings. If we try to find our beauty in physical things, like our body construction or our feelings toward an annoying little brother or sister, we'll fail miserably. But if we look to God for our self-worth, He'll help us to see what He sees in us. And He sees us for what we really are: beings made in *His* image — in His godly, beautiful image.

What is the price of two sparrows — one copper coin? But not a single sparrow can fall to the ground without your Father knowing it. And the very hairs on your head are all numbered. So don't be afraid; you are more valuable to God than a whole flock of sparrows.

Matt. 10:29-31 (NLT)

Be yourself. You don't have to copy anybody's style.
What God has given you, that's what you've got to use.
And don't try to be anyone but yourself.

Tony Dungy, *QUIET STRENGTH*

So much great art has been inspired by God, but . . .
we are God's greatest masterpiece.

Bear Rinehart
CHRISTIANMUSICTODAY.COM INTERVIEW

My mom always tells me
that imperfections equal beauty.
All of us are imperfect.

Miley Cyrus

Serving Others Serves Us, Too

Did you know that deadly alligators, when they're eating a meal, will hold another alligator's food for him so he can get a good bite? Or that an ostrich dad will go out and bring food back for his wife so she can watch the kids? Who knows if these animals are serving their loved ones out of love for God or out of survival instinct, but you get the idea. Serving others isn't hard. It's finding everyday ways to love others. Or it's finding bigger ways, if you feel God is asking you to. The point is to devote your actions to following God's will for you and then look for ways to put others ahead of yourself. When we serve others, we find that God Himself serves us. That's a pretty good deal!

Do your work with enthusiasm.
Work as if you were serving the Lord, not as if
you were serving only men and women.

Eph. 6:7 (NCV)

*Do all the good you can, by all the means you can,
in all the ways you can, in all the places you can, at all
the times you can, to all the people you can,
as long as ever you can.*

John Wesley

*Believe in something larger than yourself . . .
Get involved in the big ideas of your time.*

Barbara Bush

*When we make the decision early on in our lives
that the only thing that matters is whether or not we have done
the work of Christ, then He will make something great
out of our lives no matter what we do for a living.*

Matt Hammitt

CHRISTIANMUSICTODAY.COM INTERVIEW

I want to be God's hands and feet.

Sara Groves

TODAY'S CHRISTIAN WOMAN

Temptation Happens to Everyone

Temptations can be tiny — like taking a quarter for the vending machine off someone's desk when they're not looking. Temptations can be terrible — like using a stolen credit card to buy a new laptop. No one is immune to temptation, and every person on this planet has given in to temptation many, many times. With practice and, more importantly, with help from God, people get better at resisting things that are unhealthy for them. It takes time and maturity. Even the most mature of adults, as Paul addresses in Romans, chapter 7, struggle with sin and temptation. Fortunately, God loves us, no matter what. He just asks that we keep on trying.

Sin shall not be your master,
because you are not under law,
but under grace.

Rom. 6:14 (NIV)

Good habits result from resisting temptation.

Proverb

*Temptations, when we meet them at first, are as the lion
that roared upon Samson; but if we overcome them,
the next time we see them we shall find
a nest of honey within them.*

John Bunyan

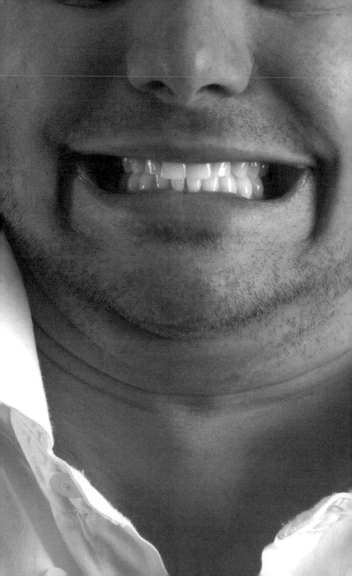

Trouble Happens

Trouble comes. There's no avoiding it — it's part of life! The difference between those who know God and those who don't is the hope that followers of Jesus have, even in times of trouble. It's true that God will never, ever allow something to happen that He can't turn into something beautiful. In the middle of trouble, it's hard to see that sometimes. But hold on to whatever tiny bit of hope you've got, and eventually the good will outshine the bad. That's a promise.

Don't be afraid, for I am with you.
Don't be discouraged, for I am your God.
I will strengthen you and help you.
I will hold you up with my victorious right hand.

Isa. 41:10 (NLT)

God's big enough to handle [it].
We don't have to have a make-believe version of life
that doesn't deal with those tough issues.

Todd Agnew
ARIZONA DAILY STAR

Even in the darkest experiences, we can see how God
can take them and demonstrate His grace
by transforming them into something beautiful.

Josh Havens
CHRISTIANMUSICTODAY.COM INTERVIEW

God will mend a broken heart if you give Him all the pieces.

Myrtie Stanton

If you want rainbows, you have to put up with the rain.

Dolly Parton

When I was nine, I did my first race — a 400-meter —
and finished last. But that taught me I didn't have to win.
I could learn just as much or more from not winning,
such as how to do it better next time.

Jackie Joyner-Kersee, Olympic gold medalist
TODAY'S CHRISTIAN WOMAN INTERVIEW

Truth Can't Be Changed

God promised us that there would be a whole lot of people in this world who lie, cheat, and steal to get our votes. That doesn't just go for politicians — it goes for religious figures, too. Many people try to use some version of Christianity to get people's attention. But the Bible and the Holy Spirit can guide you toward the real truth. And no matter what others say or do, the character of God — the truth of Jesus Christ — can't be changed. By anyone, at any time. Stick with what you know to be true, and you'll be just fine.

The Spirit shows what is true and will come
and guide you into the full truth.
The Spirit doesn't speak on his own.
He will tell you only what he has heard
from me and he will let you know
what is going to happen.

John 16:13 (CEV)

I will soon die, as everyone must.
But deep in your hearts you know that the LORD
has kept every promise he ever made
to you. Not one of them has been broken.

Josh. 23:14 (CEV)

It doesn't matter what color that candle's made of —
it's the light and the heat the draws people in.
You've probably heard it said, "All truth is God's truth."
I would add that all beauty is beautiful because
it reflects God's glory.

Jeffrey Overstreet, GRASPING FOR THE WIND

Truth is like the sun.
You can shut it out for a time,
but it ain't goin' away.

Elvis Presley

Jesus is there for us in the scriptures. How often do we ignore
Him? We must shake off this indifference. Only the faith and
the wisdom of the Church can save us, but it requires men
and women, warriors ready to risk their good names,
even their very lives to stand up for the truth.

Jim Caviezel

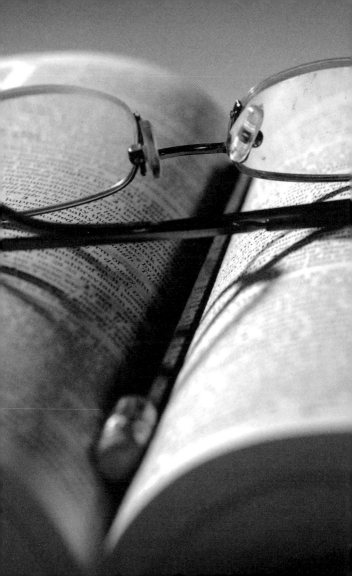

Wisdom Is Precious

One of the best gifts ever given was to King Solomon, David's son. God basically said to him, "I'll grant you one wish, Solomon. Anything you want." And instead of wealth or fame, Solomon asked for wisdom in guiding the people. He was afraid he'd do a bad job without God's help. God valued that choice so much that he gave Solomon not just more wisdom than anyone before or since, but *also* wealth and fame. Wisdom is precious. It helps you make good decisions. It means you've experienced enough to know why a good choice is a good one. And it can only come from God. As He promises, if you ask for something with a right heart, you'll get it. So if you ask for wisdom, and mean to honor Him with it, He'll give it to you.

No one is like the wise person
who can understand what things mean.
Wisdom brings happiness;
it makes sad faces happy.

Eccl. 8:1 (NCV)

Our past often prepares us for the future if we allow it to.
God provides us with opportunities to learn
from those things that have happened to us.

Tony Dungy, QUIET STRENGTH

In our everyday lives, God sometimes uses experiences
to teach us things we wouldn't have understood until we've
been through it. I was talking with a pastor friend of mine. . . .
And he said to me, "When you're in school, you go through the
lessons in class and then take your test. You don't always
understand the purpose of the lessons until you go through
the test, and that's when you're glad you took notes."

Matthew West, CHRISTIANMUSICTODAY.COM INTERVIEW

Worship Means Showing God You Mean It

Music is powerful. It seems to reach us inside, in places that words or actions can't touch. And music is one of those ways that we often use to worship God. When we drop everything — even our own self-consciousness, fear, ego, or interests — and focus all of our attention on appreciating who God is and what He's done for us, that's worship. Worship can happen by singing or praying silently. It can mean sitting in a beautiful park and enjoying the colors or standing on a mountain in the desert and shouting. Worship is any way that you can show God you love Him.

Then Moses and the people of Israel
sang this song to the Lord:
"I will sing to the Lord, for he has triumphed
gloriously; he has hurled both horse
and rider into the sea.
The Lord is my strength and my song;
he has given me victory. This is my God,
and I will praise him — my father's God,
and I will exalt him!"

Exod. 15:1-2 (NLT)

The universe itself is acting like a worship leader
for the human race if we just take time to look around us and
look above us. It always causes my heart to feel greater things
and my mind to think of higher things, of God, and His Majesty
and His creativity and everything about Him.

Phil Wickham, **BREATHECAST.COM INTERVIEW**

There's a verse in Romans, Chapter 12, that says, "Brothers,
in view of God's mercy, offer your bodies as a living sacrifice
that is holy and pleasing to God." It goes on to say,
"This is your spiritual act of worship." We honor God by
offering our bodies as living sacrifices to Him.
In other words, we say no to sin and say yes to what
God would have us to do. [It's] saying no to our own selfish
desires and saying, "God, I'm going to do what
you want me to do." That's worship.

Mac Powell

We may ignore, but we can nowhere evade, the presence
of God. The world is crowded with Him.
He walks everywhere incognito.
And the incognito is not always easy to penetrate.
The real labor is to remember to attend.
In fact to come awake. Still more to remain awake.

C.S. Lewis, *LETTERS TO MALCOLM*

If you have enjoyed this book
or it has touched your life in some way,
Hallmark would love to hear from you.

Please send your comments to:
Book Feedback
2501 McGee St., Mail Drop 215
Kansas City, MO 64108

or e-mail us at:
booknotes@hallmark.com